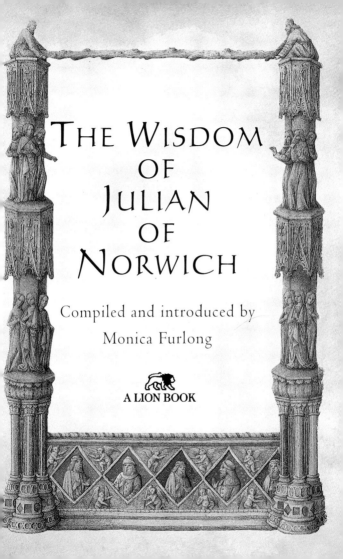

THE WISDOM
OF
JULIAN
OF
NORWICH

Compiled and introduced by
Monica Furlong

A LION BOOK

This edition copyright © 1996 Lion Publishing

Published by
Lion Publishing plc
Sandy Lane West, Oxford, England
www.lion-publishing.co.uk
ISBN 0 7459 3645 8

First edition 1996
10 9 8 7 6 5 4 3

Text acknowledgments
Reprinted from *Julian of Norwich* by Edmund
Colledge, O.S.A. and James Walsh, S.J.
© 1978 by The Missionary Society of St. Paul
the Apostle in the State of New York.
Used by permission of Paulist Press.

Artwork acknowledgments
2/3, cover: Amanda Barlow,
All other pages: Jane Thomson

A catalogue record for this book is available
from the British Library

Printed and bound in Singapore

Picture acknowledgments
1: BL 60062 Yates Thompson 11 f.6v Mass attended by officials with a procession below,
France, Lorraine, La Sainte Abbaye (c. 1300) British Library, London/Bridgeman Art Library,
London; 2/3 and cover: Chantilly, Mus. Condé, Giraudon; 4: The Bodleian Library, Oxford
(MS. Bodl. 758, fol 87r; 8: LAM59025 Ms 545 f.164v Annunciation to the Virgin Mary,
English Lewkenor Book of Hours (15th century) Lambeth Palace Library, London/Bridgeman
Art Library, London; 11: Michael Holford; 15: The Bodleian Library, Oxford (MS. Douce 131,
fol. 126r); 19: Michael Holford; 20: Chantilly, Mus. Condé, Giraudon; 25: Chantilly, Mus.
Condé, Giraudon; 27: Michael Holford; 31: Sonia Halliday; 33: Michael Holford; 34: Chantilly
Mus. Condé, Giraudon; 41: Chantilly, Mus. Condé/Lauros-Giraudon; 43: Michael Holford

CONTENTS

INTRODUCTION

Julian of Norwich (1342–some time after 1416) lived in a particularly harsh period of English history. The Hundred Years' War, which had begun before her birth, was causing terrible suffering; there were outbreaks of the Black Death in Norwich; death and famine were apparent everywhere. The Peasants' Revolt of 1369, which emerged from acute poverty, was put down with gruesome reprisals. The local leader, Geoffrey Litster, was executed very near to Julian's cell. Writing in the midst of it all, with a mind full of compassion, and a deep questioning of why so much suffering was 'necessary', Julian had an overwhelming vision of the love of God, proclaiming, as the angels in the Bible did to the shepherds, that it was a love which 'shall be to all people'.

Julian was an anchoress, one who, with the agreement of her bishop, vowed never to leave her anchorhold, in Julian's case a hermitage by the church at Conisford, a district of Norwich. It was not a very uncommon way of life in the late Middle Ages. An anchoress often had the use of two or three rooms and a garden, and a servant to obtain food and other necessaries. She would keep strict hours of prayer and practise some form of handicraft to keep herself. Sitting at a window, probably behind a curtain, she would act as a counsellor to local people who needed spiritual help and advice. Another religious woman, Margery Kempe, reports meeting Julian in just this way, and finding great consolation in their conversation.

The point of the confined life of the anchorhold was, paradoxically, to have space: space for prayer, to think about the things of God and, in Julian's case, to have an overwhelming vision of the crucified Christ.

In a sense Julian volunteered herself to enter more deeply into the mystery of meaning than most people would dare. Believing that Christ's crucifixion was central to comprehending the relationship between God and humanity, she prayed for a 'recollection' of it, what we might describe as a 'total immersion' in it. What she wanted was to see Christ on the cross for herself, as Mary Magdalen and others

had seen him. She prayed, too, for a personal experience of suffering, bodily and mental, and, finally, she asked to be granted to feel a huge longing for God, and to have that appetite satisfied, if that was God's will. As time went on, Julian tells us, she forgot about the first two requests, but the third 'remained there continually'.

When, at the age of 'thirty and a half', she suddenly developed a desperately serious illness, she seems not to have thought of it as the answer to her prayer. She was so near to death that her mother, who was sitting by her, believed she had died, and went to close her eyes, but really Julian was undergoing the actual experience of Christ's death that she had asked for. It was, of course, horrific, but gradually the horror turned into a vision of Christ triumphant and joyful. In the course of it all Julian pondered deeply on questions of evil and suffering, of salvation and damnation, of human goodness and wickedness and, above all, of the infinite love and compassion of God.

She was later to write about her 'showings' in two books—the Short Text (ST), as we now call it, which she wrote immediately after she recovered, and the Long Text (LT), which was a reworking of it all twenty years later, when her theological and spiritual contemplation of the event had matured. I have quoted from both texts. What strikes me again each time I read them is the wonderful sanity of Julian—a sort of modern Job—as she struggles with the terrible issues of pain and suffering and evil, determined to work out, if she can, how they can be compatible with God's love. She wants answers. Her struggle emerges from a love and sympathy with suffering humanity, her longing to see people delivered from their pain and sorrow and released into the joy of God. Her own hard-won awareness is that 'all shall be well, all manner of things shall be well.'

MONICA FURLONG

March 1996

THE WORLD
AND THE SOUL

The World Sustained by God

Our Lord showed me a spiritual sight of his
familiar love. I saw that he is to us everything
which is good and comforting for our help.
He is our clothing, for he is that love which
wraps and enfolds us, embraces us and guides
us, surrounds us for his love, which is so
tender that he may never desert us. And so in
this sight I saw truly that he is everything
which is good, as I understand. And in this he
showed me something small, no bigger than a
hazelnut, lying in the palm of my hand, and I
perceived that it was as round as any ball. I
looked at it and thought: What can this be?
And I was given this general answer: It is
everything which is made. I was amazed that it
could last, for I thought that it was so little
that it could suddenly fall into nothing. And I
was answered in my understanding: It lasts and
always will, because God loves it; and thus
everything has being through the love of God.

Showings. ST. Chapter 4

WORLDLY DISTRACTIONS

This is the reason why those who deliberately
occupy themselves with earthly business,
constantly seeking worldly well-being, have not
God's rest in their hearts; for they love and
seek their rest in this thing which is so little
and in which there is no rest, and do not know
God who is almighty, all wise and all good.
God wishes to be known, and it pleases him
that we should rest in him; for all things which
are beneath him are not sufficient for us.

ST. Chapter 4

PARTNERSHIP WITH GOD

Prayer unites the soul to God, for although the soul may always be like God in nature and substance, it is often unlike him in condition, through human sin. Prayer makes the soul like God when the soul wills as God wills; then it is like God in condition, as it is in nature. And so he teaches us to pray and to have firm trust that we shall have what we pray for, because everything which is done would be done, even though we had never prayed for it. But God's love is so great that he regards us as partners in his good work; and so he moves us to pray for what it pleases him to do, for whatever prayer or good desire comes to us by his gift he will repay us for, and give us eternal reward.

ST. Chapter 19

RESTING IN GOD

[Sometimes] it seems to the soul that God has been moved to look upon it, as though it had been in pain or in prison, saying: I am glad that you have found rest, for I have always loved you and I love you now, and you love me.

ST. Chapter 19

5

CHOOSING GOD

It is God's will that we accept his commands and his consolations as generously and as fully as we are able; and he also wants us to accept our tarrying and our suffering as lightly as we are able, and to count them as nothing. For the more lightly we accept them, the less importance we ascribe to them because of our love, the less pain shall we experience from them and the more thanks shall we have for them. In this blessed revelation I was truly taught that any man or woman who voluntarily chooses God in his lifetime may be sure that he too is chosen.

ST. Chapter 20

JESUS IN US

Our Lord opened my spiritual eyes, and
showed me my soul in the midst of my heart. I
saw my soul as wide as if it were a kingdom,
and from the state in which I saw it, it seemed
to me as if it were a fine city. In the midst of
this sits our Lord Jesus, true God and true
man, a handsome person and tall, honourable,
the greatest lord. And I saw him splendidly clad
in honours. He sits erect there in the soul, in
peace and rest, and he rules and he guards
heaven and earth and everything that is. The
humanity and the divinity sit at rest, and the
divinity rules and guards, without instruments
or effort. And my soul is blessedly occupied by
the divinity, sovereign power, sovereign wisdom,
sovereign goodness. The place which Jesus
takes in our soul he will nevermore vacate, for
in us is his home of homes, and it is the
greatest delight for him to dwell there.

ST. Chapter 22

'You Will Not Be Overcome'

These words: You will not be overcome, were
said very insistently and strongly [by Jesus],
for certainty and strength against every
tribulation which may come. He did not say:
You will not be assailed, you will not be
belaboured, you will not be disquieted, but he
said: You will not be overcome.

ST. Chapter 22

DESIRE

GOD ALONE IS ENOUGH

God, of your goodness give me yourself, for you
are enough for me, and I can ask for nothing
which is less which can pay you full worship.
And if I ask anything which is less, always I am
in want; but only in you do I have everything.

LT. Chapter 5

GOD'S LOVE—OUR FULFILMENT

There is no created being who can know how much and how sweetly and how tenderly the Creator loves us. And therefore we can with his grace and his help persevere in spiritual contemplation, with endless wonder at this high, surpassing, immeasurable love which our Lord in his goodness has for us; and therefore we may with reverence ask from our lover all that we will, for our natural will is to have God, and God's good will is to have us, and we can never stop willing or loving until the time comes that we shall be filled full in heaven.

LT. Chapter 6

LOVE IS MORE THAN VISIONS

I am not good because of [my] revelations, but only if I love God better; and inasmuch as you love God better, it is more to you than to me. I do not say this to those who are wise, because they know it well. But I say it to you who are simple, to give you comfort and strength; for we are all one in love, for truly it was not revealed to me that God loves me better than the humblest soul who is in a state of grace. For I am sure that there are many who never had revelations or visions, but only the common teaching of Holy Church, who love God better than I. If I pay special attention to myself I am nothing at all; but in general I am, I hope, in the unity of love with all my fellow Christians.

LT Chapter 9

Safe with God

Once my understanding was let down into the bottom of the sea, and there I saw green hills and valleys, with the appearance of moss, strewn with seaweed and gravel. Then I understood in this way: that if a man or woman were there under the wide waters, if he could see God, as God is continually with man, he would be safe in soul and body, and come to no harm. And furthermore, he would have more consolation and strength than all this world can tell.

LT. Chapter 10

THREE GIFTS

It is God's will that we receive three things from him as gifts as we seek. The first is that we seek willingly and diligently without sloth, as that may be with his grace, joyfully and happily, without unreasonable depression and useless sorrow. The second is that we wait for him steadfastly, out of love for him, without grumbling and contending against him, to the end of our lives, for that will last only for a time. The third is that we have great trust in him, out of complete and true faith, for it is his will that we know that he will appear, suddenly and blessedly, to all his lovers. For he works in secret, and he will be perceived, and his appearing will be very sudden.

And he wants to be trusted, for he is very accessible, familiar and courteous, blessed may he be.

LT. Chapter 10

GOD'S FEAST

My understanding was lifted up into heaven, where I saw our Lord God as a lord in his own house, who has called all his friends to a splendid feast. Then I did not see him seated anywhere in his own house; but I saw him reign in his house as a king and fill it all full of joy and mirth, gladdening and consoling his dear friends with himself, very familiarly and courteously, with wonderful melody in endless love in his own fair blissful countenance.

LT. Chapter 14

JOY

DESOLATION AND JOY

I was changed, and abandoned to myself,
oppressed and weary of my life and ruing
myself, so that I hardly had the patience to go
on living. I felt that there was no ease or
comfort for me except faith, hope and love,
and truly I felt very little of this. And then
presently God gave me again comfort and rest
for my soul, delight and security so blessedly
and so powerfully that there was no fear, no
sorrow, no pain, physical or spiritual, that one
could suffer which might have disturbed me.
And then again I felt the pain, and then
afterwards the delight and the joy, now the one
and now the other, again and again, I suppose
about twenty times. And in the time of joy
I could have said with St. Paul: Nothing shall
separate me from the love of Christ; and in
the pain I could have said with St. Peter: Lord,
save me, I am perishing.

LT. Chapter 15

WHAT GOD HAS DONE FOR US

It is God's will that we have true delight with him in our salvation, and in it he wants us to be greatly comforted... For we are his bliss, because he endlessly delights in us; and so with his grace shall we delight in him. All that he does for us and has done and will do was never expense or labour to him, nor could it be, except only that he died in our humanity, beginning at the sweet Incarnation and lasting until his blessed Resurrection on Easter morning. So long did the labour and expense of our redemption last, in which deed he always and endlessly rejoices.

LT. Chapter 23

'I Am He'

After this our Lord showed himself to me, and
he appeared to me more glorified than I had
seen him before, in which I was taught that our
soul will never have rest till it comes into him,
acknowledging that he is full of joy, familiar
and courteous and blissful and true life. Again
and again our Lord said, I am he, I am he, I am
he who is highest. I am he whom you love.
I am he in whom you delight. I am he whom
you serve. I am he for whom you long. I am he
whom you desire. I am he whom you intend.
I am he who is all.

LT. Chapter 26

Because of the tender love which our good Lord has for all who will be saved, he comforts readily and sweetly, meaning this: It is true that sin is the cause of all this pain, but all will be well, and every kind of thing will be well. These words were revealed most tenderly, showing no kind of blame to me or to anyone who will be saved.

LT. Chapter 27

SIN

Why Sin is Allowed

I saw hidden in God an exalted and wonderful mystery, which he will make plain and we shall know in heaven. In this knowledge we shall truly see the cause why he allowed sin to come, and in this sight we shall rejoice forever.

LT. Chapter 27

LOVE FOR OTHERS

Then I saw that every natural compassion which
one has for one's fellow Christians in love is
Christ in us, and that every kind of self-
humiliation which he manifested in his Passion
was manifested again in this compassion, in
which there were two different understandings
of our Lord's intention. One was the bliss that
we are brought to, in which he wants us to
rejoice. The other is for consolation in our pain.

LT. Chapter 28

GOD THIRSTS FOR US

As truly as there is in God a quality of pity and compassion, so truly is there in God a quality of thirst and longing; and the power of this longing in Christ enables us to respond to his longing, and without this no soul comes to heaven. And this quality of longing and thirst comes from God's everlasting goodness, just as the quality of pity comes from his everlasting goodness. And though he may have both longing and pity, they are different qualities, as I see them: and this is the characteristic of spiritual thirst, which will persist in him so long as we are in need, and will draw us up into his bliss.

LT. Chapter 31

EVERYTHING PUT RIGHT

There is a deed which the blessed Trinity will perform on the last day, as I see it, and what the deed will be and how it will be performed is unknown to every creature… and it will be until the deed is done. This is the great deed ordained by our Lord God from without beginning, treasured and hidden in his blessed breast, known only to himself, through which deed he will make all things well. For just as the blessed Trinity created all things from nothing, just so will the same blessed Trinity make everything well which is not well… And all this being so, it seemed to me that it was impossible that every kind of thing should be well, as our Lord revealed at this time. And to this I had no other answer as a revelation from our Lord except this: What is impossible to you is not impossible to me. I shall preserve my word in everything, and I shall make everything well.

LT. Chapter 32

SWEET HARMONY

Everything which our Lord God does is righteous, and all which he tolerates is honourable; and in these two are good and evil comprehended. For our Lord does everything which is good, and our Lord tolerates what is evil. I do not say that evil is honourable, but I say that our Lord God's toleration is honourable, through which his goodness will be known eternally, and his wonderful meekness and mildness by this working of mercy and grace.

Righteousness is that which is so good that it cannot be better than it is, for God himself is true righteousness, and all his works are righteously performed, as they are ordained from eternity by his exalted power, his exalted wisdom, his exalted goodness. And what he has ordained for the best he constantly brings to pass in the same way, and directs to the same end... And the contemplation of this blessed harmony is most sweet to the soul which sees it by grace.

LT. Chapter 35

MERCY AND RIGHTEOUSNESS

Mercy is an operation which comes from the goodness of God, and it will go on operating so long as sin is permitted to harass righteous souls. And when sin is no longer permitted to harass, then the operation of mercy will cease. And then all will be brought into righteousness and stand fast there forever. By his toleration we fall, and in his blessed love, with his power and his wisdom, we are protected, and by mercy and grace we are raised to much more joy. And so in righteousness and in mercy he wishes to be known and loved, now and forever. And the soul that wisely contemplates in grace is well satisfied with both, and endlessly delights.

LT. Chapter 35

SIN CANNOT IMPEDE GOD

Our Lord God revealed that a deed will be done and he himself will do it, and it will be honourable and wonderful and plentiful, and it will be done with respect to me, and he himself will do it. And this is the highest joy that the soul understood, that God himself will do it, and I shall do nothing at all but sin; and my sin will not impede the operation of his goodness. And I saw that the contemplation of this is a heavenly joy in a soul which fears God and always lovingly through grace desires the will of God. This deed will be begun here, and it will be honour to God and to the plentiful profit of all his lovers on earth; and as we come to heaven each one of us will see it with wonderful joy; and it will go on operating until the last day. And the honour and the bliss of it will last in heaven before God and all his holy saints eternally.

LT. Chapter 36

GOD LOVES US AS WE ARE

Our Lord revealed this to me in the
completeness of his love, that we are standing
in his sight, yes, that he loves us now whilst
we are here as well as he will when we are
there, before his blessed face; but all our
travail is because love is lacking on our side.

LT. Chapter 37

PRAYER

A Foretaste of Joy

Prayer is a right understanding of that fulness of joy which is to come, with true longing and trust. The savouring or seeing of our bliss, to which we are ordained, by nature makes us to long; true understanding and love, with a sweet recollection in our savour by grace makes us to trust. And in these two operations our Lord constantly regards us, for this is our duty, and his goodness cannot assign any less to us than it is our obligation diligently to perform. And when we do it, still it will seem to us that it is nothing. And this is true. But let us do what we can, and meekly ask mercy and grace, and everything which is lacking in us we shall find in him. And this is what he means when he says: I am the foundation of your beseeching.

LT. Chapter 42

IMPERCEPTIBLE PRAYER

When our courteous Lord of his special grace
shows himself to our soul, we have what we
desire, and then for that time we do not see
what more we should pray for, but all our
intention and all our powers are wholly
directed to contemplating him. And as I see it,
this is an exalted and an imperceptible prayer;
for the whole reason why we pray is to be
united into the vision and contemplation of
him to whom we pray.

LT. Chapter 43

KNOWING OURSELVES AND GOD

Our passing life which we have here does not know in our senses what our self is, but we know in our faith. And when we know and see, truly and clearly, what our self is, then we shall truly and clearly see and know our Lord God in the fulness of joy. And therefore it must necessarily be that the nearer we are to bliss, the more we shall long both by nature and by grace. We may have knowledge of ourselves in this life by the continuing help and power of our exalted nature, in which knowledge we may increase and grow by the furthering and help of mercy and grace. But we may never fully know ourselves until the last moment, at which moment this passing life and every kind of pain and woe will have an end. And therefore this belongs to our properties, both by nature and by grace to long and desire with all our powers to know ourselves, in which full knowledge we shall truly and clearly know our God in the fulness of endless joy.

LT. Chapter 46

WE NEVER SHALL BE LOST

In endless love we are led and protected by God,
and we never shall be lost; for he wants us to
know that the soul is a life, which life of his
goodness and his grace will last in heaven
without end, loving him, thanking him, praising
him. And just as we were to be without end, so
we were treasured and hidden in God, known
and loved from without beginning. Therefore he
wants us to know that the noblest thing which
he ever made is mankind, and the fullest
substance and the highest power is the blessed
soul of Christ. And furthermore, he wants us to
know that this beloved soul was preciously
knitted to him in its making, by a knot so
subtle and so mighty that it is united in God.
In this uniting it is made endlessly holy.
Furthermore, he wants us to know that all the
souls which will be saved in heaven without end
are knit in this knot, and united in this union,
and made holy in this holiness.

LT. Chapter 53

GOD OUR FATHER AND MOTHER

As truly as God is our Father, so truly is God our Mother, and he revealed that in everything, and especially in these sweet words where he says I am he; that is to say: I am he, the power and greatness of fatherhood; I am he, the wisdom and the lovingness of motherhood; I am he, the light and the grace which is all blessed love; I am he, the Trinity; I am he, the unity; I am he, the great supreme goodness of every kind of thing; I am he who makes you to love; I am he who makes you to long; I am he, the endless fulfilling of all true desires.

LT. Chapter 59